SCHIRMER'S LIBRARY
OF MUSICAL CLASSICS

FELIX MENDELSSOHN-BARTHOLDY

Concertos
For the Piano

With the Orchestral Accompaniments
Arranged for a Second Piano by
ADOLF RUTHARDT

→ Op. 25, in G minor — Library Vol. 61

Op. 40, in D minor — Library Vol. 62

G. SCHIRMER, Inc.

DISTRIBUTED BY

HAL•LEONARD®
CORPORATION
7777 W. BLUEMOUND RD. P.O. BOX 13819 MILWAUKEE, WI 53213

Concerto I.

F. MENDELSSOHN. Op.25.
Composed 1882.
Published May, 1833.

*) The "Tutti" may be executed by both players.

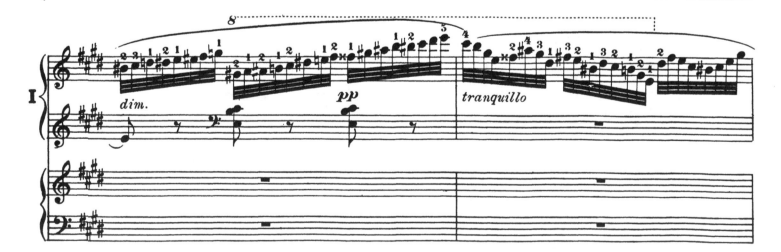

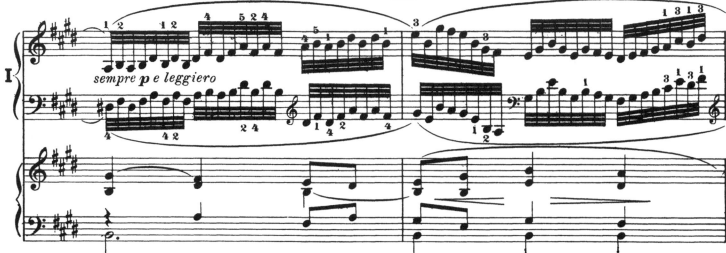

26

Presto.

15720

Solo

Molto allegro e vivace.

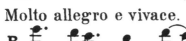

Molto allegro e vivace.

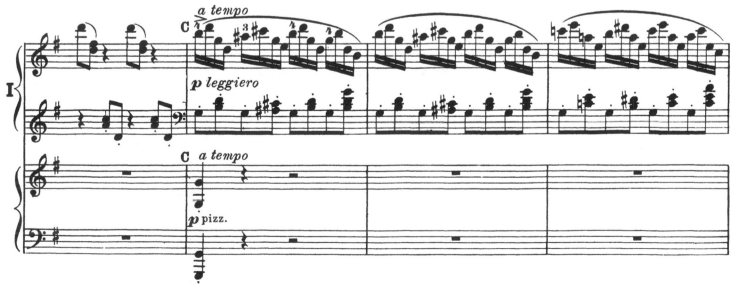

30

15730

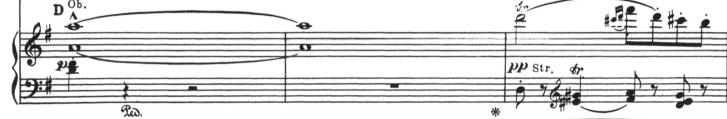

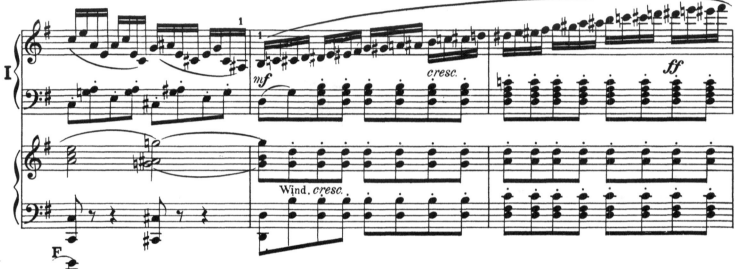

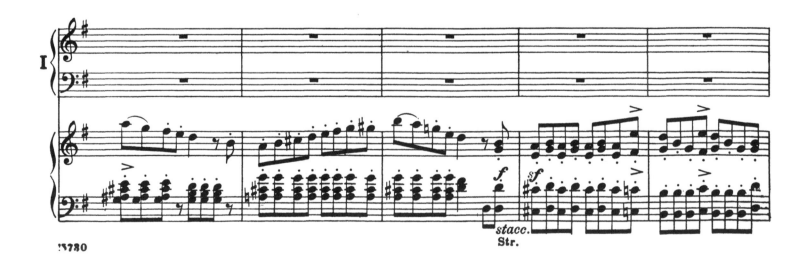